Navigating you
with faith-f

7 BIBLICAL TRUTHS
FOR TEENAGERS

DR. GARRETT D. NOGAN

Copyright © 2024 by Garrett Nogan.

All Scripture quotations, unless otherwise indicated, are taken from the Holy Bible, New International Version®, NIV®. Copyright ©1973, 1978, 1984, 2011 by Biblica, Inc.™ Used by permission of Zondervan. All rights reserved worldwide. www.zondervan.com The "NIV" and "New International Version" are trademarks registered in the United States Patent and Trademark Office by Biblica, Inc.™

Scripture quotations marked NLT are taken from the Holy Bible, New Living Translation, copyright © 1996, 2004, 2015 by Tyndale House Foundation. Used by permission of Tyndale House Publishers, Inc., Carol Stream, Illinois 60188. All rights reserved.

Scripture quotations marked MSG are taken from The Message, copyright © 1993, 2002, 2018 by Eugene H. Peterson. Used by permission of NavPress. All rights reserved. Represented by Tyndale House Publishers.

Scripture quotations marked ESV are from the ESV® Bible (The Holy Bible, English Standard Version®), © 2001 by Crossway, a publishing ministry of Good News Publishers. Used by permission. All rights reserved. The ESV text may not be quoted in any publication made available to the public by a Creative Commons license. The ESV may not be translated in whole or in part into any other language.

"Where was this when I was in middle/high school? Where was this when I parented my kids through their school years? At least I have it now. This devotional identifies the core wrestling we all do, and it beautifully points us to anchor our hearts and lives in Jesus in the midst of these wrestlings. Garrett is tenderly honest and necessarily direct while dealing with difficult subjects. This is a must read for every teen. And then it's a must reread for every teen as well!"

Dave D'Angelo
Lead Pastor, North Way Christian Community

"Life can be challenging for modern teens who are attempting to navigate complex relationships, feelings, and pressures that come with social media and expectations from society. Yet, there is hope for all young people who choose to seek purpose and meaning in life through a relationship with Jesus. In this excellent resource for teens, Dr. Garrett Nogan provides practical solutions straight from the Bible for teens to apply to their lives. This helpful book offers an invitation into something beautiful that all young people can experience. I will encourage the young people in my life to read it regularly to remind them of the promises and opportunities that the Lord presents to all of us."

Dr. Bryan McCabe
President, Bakke Graduate University

CONTENTS

Introduction	1
Day 1 – Be You	3
Day 2 – God Has a Plan for You	7
Day 3 – Don't Conform	11
Day 4 - God's Presence > Anxiety	15
Day 5 - Find Your Identity and Worth in Christ	19
Day 6 - People-Pleasing, Approval of Others, and Fear of Man	25
Day 7 - You Can Do Anything You Want To, but Not Everything Is Good for You	29
Conclusion	34

INTRODUCTION

I grew up in a loving Christian home, but like many teenagers (and maybe you), I strayed from the Lord and got pretty off track. And while it's been about twenty years since I've been a teen, not all that much has changed. What I struggled with then and what you're going through now might not be all that different.

I struggled with peer pressure and fitting in. *You too?*

I struggled with being a Christian and living out my faith. *You too?*

I struggled with liking who God made me. *You too?*

I struggled with confidence, identity, and self-worth. *You too?*

I struggled with comparison, insecurities, and anxiety. *You too?*

See, we're not all that different.

Looking back now, I wish there had been a book or a short devotional that could have helped me work through some of these things from a biblical perspective—six or seven really solid biblical truths to help keep me on track.

I've worked with thousands of teenagers over the past ten to twelve years, both in my full-time job as a college counselor and as a student ministry/youth volunteer at my church. And in my role as a Christian social media "influencer," a big chunk of my half million followers are teens. So, this short devotional was written by someone very much in tune with what teenagers are going through, and it's my prayer that these seven biblical truths will encourage you, empower you, strengthen your relationship with God, and quite possibly change your life.

DAY 1
Be You

We're going to dive right in if that's okay with you . . .

Cool.

Are there some things you don't really like about yourself? Attributes, qualities, and traits other people have that you wish you had? Maybe their personality, their athletic ability, their confidence, their smarts, their body, their friendliness, their popularity, and so forth. Ever say to yourself, "If only I could be like that person . . ."?

(Told ya we're going to dive right in.)

I get it. I've struggled with this too. *Mightily*. Still do sometimes if I'm being honest.

Comparison and coveting—wanting what other people have and breaking the tenth commandment—is a massively dangerous trap that will rob you of joy, peace, and contentment (satisfaction), and it will keep you from becoming who God *uniquely* created and called you to be.

Jesus said in John 10:10 that the enemy comes to steal,

kill, and destroy. The enemy wants nothing more than to *steal* the person God created you to be, *kill* the unique gifts, skills, and calling God has placed on you, and *destroy* an abundant and peace-filled future. He does this by stirring up comparison and coveting, and by feeding you lies that you're not good enough, not cool enough, not smart enough, not athletic enough, not funny enough . . . not ENOUGH.

There were many things I didn't necessarily like about myself growing up. To be honest, I kind of thought I was a loser in some ways. But I didn't see the full picture. There were gifts, skills, and abilities God *uniquely* placed in me that took a little while to fully develop. They weren't revealed until later in my life as I got older and my relationship with God grew. Is it possible that if you keep growing in your relationship with God you might also get a clearer picture of who you are in His eyes? Keep growing in your relationship with Him. That's your job. God will take care of the rest.

Trust in the truth of Psalm 139:14: "I praise you because I am *fearfully* and *wonderfully* made." I've heard it said that the "wonderfully made" part of that verse refers to us being attractively, beautifully, cleverly, and neatly constructed, shaped, and formed by God. That's pretty cool. And amazing. And encouraging! We're meant to be unique and different from each other. It'd be kind of boring if we were all the same . . . at least I think so. The New Living Translation refers to us as being "wonderfully complex"! Up to this point in life, is it possible you've only been focusing on the "complex" part of who you are and not the "wonderful" part? ☺

(Just to be clear, this doesn't mean you get to "do you" and "live your truth" and act on every urge and desire you have. That is very much *not* what I'm saying here, and it's not what God is referring to in this verse.)

I know sometimes it's hard to see and feel it, but you *are* fearfully made, wonderfully made, uniquely made, and beautifully made, my friend. Your strengths, "weaknesses" (God uses our weaknesses), personality, and giftings were handcrafted on purpose by God. **The more you try to be like other people, the further you get from becoming the person God created *you* to be.**

There is so much freedom and easiness (and less stress and pressure!) in simply being you. Don't try to be anyone else. Don't try to be like me. Don't try to be like that popular kid in school. Don't try to be like an influencer you watch on social media. Be you.

Notes

DAY 2
God Has a Plan for You

Ever wonder what the meaning of life is? Or why you exist? Or what's the purpose of all this?

Maybe you've asked yourself, "How am I supposed to know what to do with my life?"

I struggled with this a lot as a teenager. And to be completely open with you, I still struggle with this one from time to time. That comes from someone who now has a successful career. Someone who's an author, a doctor, a worship leader, and a small-group Bible study leader. Someone with multiple faith-based social media ministries. Someone who seemingly "has it all together." I hope that's a little comforting to you—you're not alone.

But that's what the enemy does. He likes to plant lies in our minds (John 10:10) so you and I doubt the goodness of God and His plans for us. Yet all throughout Scripture, God reminds us that He *does* have good plans and purposes for us.

Jeremiah 29:11 says, "'For I know the plans I have for you,' says the LORD. 'They are plans for good and not for disaster, to give you a future and hope'" (NLT). This verse doesn't mean you're going to be a millionaire or a CEO or a professional basketball player. You might if that's part of God's plan for you. **But more so, this verse gives us reassurance and hope and confidence that God *does* have a plan for us, and it's *good*.** And we can trust Him even if we don't understand or know the details (which we often won't!).

Ephesians 2:10 says, "For we are God's handiwork [masterpiece], created in Christ Jesus to do good works, which God prepared in advance for us to do." God has good works, good plans, and good purposes prepared for you and me. Wow, that's reassuring and comforting, isn't it? Let's commit our ways and our hearts to Him so we can walk in those plans and purposes.

I love what Paul says in Philippians 1:6. Check it out on your own, but let me loosely paraphrase the verse and speak it directly to you: "I, Garrett Nogan, am personally confident that God began a good work in you (yes, you reading this) long ago, and He will continue to grow and complete and perfect that plan in and through your life for His glory."

Listen—God has a plan for you. Yes, *you*.

Life can be confusing and challenging as a teen. Sometimes it can seem pointless, meaningless, or even hopeless (been there). But trust the promises of God in the verses above. And remember that God has plans and purposes for you to be used—your gifts, your personality, your strengths, and even your weaknesses—for His kingdom and His glory. And as a result, you will help many people. Don't let the enemy steal that. Trust God. He has a plan. And it's GOOD.

Notes

DAY 3
Don't Conform

Romans 12:2 says, "Do not conform to the pattern of this world . . ."

I failed at this one. Big time. I had lukewarm (casual) faith in high school and college, and the temptations of the world, peer pressure, and "trying to fit in" got the best of me. I got completely swept up in the party scene and everything it involves—all the things that seemed right at the time but came with brutal consequences down the road. Proverbs 14:12 says, "There is a way that appears to be right, but in the end it leads to death." Yep. Right on. **It seemed *right* to me at the time.** But in the long run, it led to destruction. It led to *years* of anxiety, depression, insecurities, lack of confidence, sexual impurity, people-pleasing, fear of man, and more.

I listened to Pastor Craig Groeschel a lot when I was turning from my lifestyle of sin and really getting to know God. Something he said has always stuck with me and I'll paraphrase here:

"Sin can be fun for a while. It can be a fun ride. But when

the ride is over, you've got a massive mess on your hands to clean up."

Maybe partying and getting involved in that scene isn't a temptation for you to "conform" to. If so, praise God! But maybe it's something else. Maybe it's conforming to the world in terms of swearing because "everyone uses that language." Maybe it's conforming to the world in terms of what you wear because "everyone's wearing it." Maybe it's watching and looking at things on a screen that you shouldn't, but "everyone's doing it." Maybe it's peer pressure to do something you know is wrong—lying, cheating, stealing, gossiping, bullying, and so on.

Here's a general rule of thumb: Whatever the world and culture is doing, we as Christians do the opposite. We're countercultural.

I really love *The Message* and NLT versions of Romans 12:2:

"Don't become so well-adjusted to your culture that you fit into it without even thinking. Instead, fix your attention on God. You'll be changed from the inside out. Readily recognize what he wants from you, and quickly respond to it. Unlike the culture around you, always dragging you down to its level of immaturity, God brings the best out of you, develops well-formed maturity in you" (Romans 12:2 MSG).

"Don't copy the behavior and customs of this world, but let God transform you into a new person by changing the way you think. Then you will learn to know God's will for you, which is good and pleasing and perfect" (Romans 12:2 NLT).

You might be reading this and thinking, "Garrett, it's too late. I've already given in to temptation." It's okay! God's got you! He still loves you. He's still chasing after you. He still wants a relationship with you. And the amazing thing is, God will redeem and restore our past and our stupidity. I'm living proof, writing this devotional. And as Romans 8:28 says, He will use it for your good. If He did it for me, He can do it for you. Commit your life and ways to Him.

And, hey, if you've been standing strong in your beliefs and not conforming to the patterns of this world . . . I'm so proud of you. And so is God! Keep it up!

The culture and the world will drag you down. Don't copy them. Don't imitate them. Don't try to fit in. You are called higher.

Notes

DAY 4
God's Presence > Anxiety

Listen. I *personally* understand the pain, suffering, and agony of anxiety. The pit in your stomach. Constant jitters. Uneasiness. Feeling on edge. Sleepless nights. Racing thoughts. Racing heart. Trying to catch your breath. I get it. All of it. I struggled with it significantly in my twenties, and it still surfaces from time to time in my life. I understand it so much that I wrote a twenty-one day prayer devotional on it a few years ago.

But I also *personally* understand the reality and the peace of Psalm 94:19: "When anxiety was great within me, your consolation brought me joy."

The word *consolation* means comfort and presence.

I tried a lot of things to help me with anxiety. Drinking. Manifesting. Worldly affirmations. Endless Google and YouTube searches. The only thing that brought me true comfort and peace and hope and healing was (and still is) God's presence.

Getting into God's presence . . . what did this look like

for me, and how might you be able to do it?

The biggest thing for me has been listening to worship music. I can't tell you how many nights after work and the gym (physical activity is also important to fight anxiety), I would come home, eat dinner, and then just lie on my couch listening to worship music with the lights off and no other distractions for hours. Sometimes it might be for only ten minutes. And sometimes the lights might be on. **Lights don't matter. Length of time doesn't matter. God's presence matters.** James 4:8 says, "Draw near to God, and he will draw near to you" (ESV).

I would do this a ton, and I continue to do it even now. It was the only thing that seemed to bring any sort of comfort and peace. I would lie there and let the truth and power of the lyrics, often based directly on Scripture, soak into my mind. And sometimes I might even fall asleep. In the *comfort*, *presence*, and arms of my loving Father.

I would also do "mini sessions" like this throughout my day and still do. Sitting in my car in a parking lot a few minutes before heading into work. Sitting in my car in a parking lot for a few minutes during my lunch break. Sitting in my car a few minutes before church, or the doctor's office, or the gym, or Bible study, or wherever I was going. A lot of sacred time was spent in my car sitting in parking lots with God!

Listening to worship music obviously isn't the only way to get into God's presence, but it's been the best and most powerful way for me. It helped me practice Psalm 46:10, "Be still and know that I am God," and Exodus 14:14, "The LORD will fight for you; you need only be still." And it pointed me to read and study the living and active "owner's manual for life"–the Bible. I encourage you to do the same. There's something special and sacred about being still and letting God fight the battle going on within you.

Maybe it takes a little trial and error to find what works best for you and your daily schedule. But get into God's presence. Multiple times a day. **Let His presence and comfort bring you joy and hope and peace amid your anxiety.**

Notes

DAY 5
Find Your Identity and Worth in Christ

Nick Vujicic, a well-known Christian evangelist who was born without arms or legs, says, "If you put your happiness in temporary things your happiness will be temporary."

Read that again.

Where do you get your identity and self-worth? In other words, where do you find your confidence, self-esteem, and happiness?

I struggled with this for years because, as Nick Vujicic said, **I put my happiness in temporary things**. As a teenager, I found my identity and worth in a number of things—basketball, grades, relationships, popularity, and parties, just to name a few.

Basketball . . . I played basketball growing up and always loved it. I practiced a ton but never made more than the junior varsity team. My older brother started on the varsity team as a freshman. I just wasn't *good enough* . . .

Grades . . . I was never super smart. I always had to work really hard and study way more than other people. My brothers made it look effortless. My older brother (the one who started varsity as a freshman) was top of his class. My younger brother was valedictorian. I just wasn't *smart enough* . . .

Relationships . . . I dated around a bit in high school, but honestly, I never got "the girl." I never got the girl I wanted. I tried and tried and tried. All I got was rejection. Must not have been *attractive enough* . . .

Popularity . . . I had a lot of different friends as a teenager, but I always felt like I was on the outside looking in when it came to the "in crowd." Must not have been *cool enough* . . .

Parties . . . I started doing this midway through high school and got much of the same result. It was temporarily fun and filling. But it was just that—temporary. And it left me empty, anxious, and depressed.

In Matthew 7:24-25, Jesus says, "Everyone who hears these words of mine and acts on them will be like the wise man who built his house on the rock. The rain fell, and the torrents raged, and the wind blew and beat against that house; but it did not fall because its foundation was on the rock."

Jeremiah 17:7-8 tells us, "But blessed is the one who trusts in the Lord, whose confidence [identity] is in him. They will be like a tree planted by the water that sends out its roots by the stream. It does not fear when heat comes; its leaves are always green. It has no worries in a year of drought and never fails to bear fruit."

If you put your happiness, identity, and worth in temporary things—school, sports, performance, relationships, how funny you are, how athletic you are, how attractive you are, how popular you are, what college you got into—your happiness will be temporary.

And, hey, if you have been bullied or currently are being bullied, I'm so sorry. I'm so sorry you're going through that. **But please remember that your identity, worth, and value are not in what other people say about you.** God says you are loved, chosen, adored, and enough. You can be secure in Him. And please let someone know if you are being bullied. There is more help these days than ever.

Listen—if this devotional I wrote (the one you're reading right now) turns out to be a total flop, it's okay—my identity is secure in Christ.

If you didn't make the team, the club, or the school play, it's okay—your identity is secure in Christ.

If you didn't win the track meet or had a bad game, it's okay—your identity is secure in Christ.

If you didn't make AP honors or get the scores you hoped for on the SAT, ACT, or any other test, it's okay—your identity is secure in Christ.

If you got laughed at for being a Christian, or for focusing on school, or for not conforming to whatever peer pressure is going on, it's okay—*your identity is secure in Christ.*

I could go down the list for a while here, but you get the point.

Build your life and identity on God so that when the storms and rains and challenges of life come, your foundation is unshaken.

Notes

DAY 6
People-Pleasing, Approval of Others, and Fear of Man

Do you find yourself constantly (or even just from time to time) seeking the acceptance and approval of others? Your friends, teachers, coaches, or peers? Trying to impress them or win them over in your interactions throughout the day? Trying to earn your worth and acceptance from others? Maybe trying to impress them with how smart you are, how funny you are, or how cool you are? *Trying* to fit in . . .

If that's you, welcome to the 49 Percent Club. And it's not a good club. A 2023 study showed that 49 percent of Americans identify as people-pleasers and are highly concerned with what other people think of them. Don't worry though—I'm in that club with you (I'm a work in progress just like you). So is every other person you see today . . . literally every other person.

This is called fear of man.

It can be a crippling cycle.

Let's break free from it.

I want to arm you with three powerful verses that have helped me significantly over the years with the need to please people, impress them, and earn acceptance and approval from them.

In Galatians 1:10, Paul says, "For am I now seeking the approval of man, or of God? Or am I trying to please man? If I were still trying to please man, I would not be a servant of Christ" (ESV).

Jesus tells us in John 5:41, "I do not receive glory from people" (ESV).

And Proverbs 29:25 says, "The fear of human opinion disables; trusting in GOD protects you from that" (MSG).

Powerful.

These verses have allowed me to be *concerned* about what people think of me, but not *consumed* by what people think of me. It's okay to be concerned and aware of what other people think of you and how you're coming across. That's called social and emotional intelligence. It's a good thing. That's how we grow and improve. But it's not okay to be mentally and emotionally *consumed* by what other people think of you. That's not healthy. And it's not what God wants for you.

Remember the Romans 12:2 verse we talked about earlier? The one about not conforming to the world? The second half of that verse says to be transformed (changed) by the renewing of your mind. If fear of man is something you struggle with, renew your mind with this biblical truth throughout the day: "I don't seek approval, acceptance, and glory from other people, only from God."

I actually have these verses at my work desk on sticky notes so I can remind myself of this truth throughout the day. I've gone through seasons where fear of man is so prevalent and consuming that I put these verses as wallpaper on my phone. We look at our phones over 160 times a day. Not a bad thing to renew your mind with 160 times a day . . .

Reminding yourself of these verses will eventually free you to embrace what we learned on Day 1: to just BE YOU. Remember, you have an audience of *One*.

Notes

DAY 7
You Can Do Anything You Want To, but Not Everything Is Good for You

I'd consider myself a pretty encouraging guy. Hopefully you've felt that in these pages. But I need to get in your space here for a minute to challenge and call you higher.

Social media is a beautiful thing. While I've never been obsessed with it (odd for someone with a large following), I love the access it gives me to sermons, podcasts, pastors, fitness, music, and tons of other things to help me grow as a person and believer. I love that I can comment on posts and pictures from friends and family. And I also love the fact that TikTok and Instagram entertain me and give me a good laugh from time to time!

But too much of anything (not including God) can be a bad thing (Proverbs 25:16).

Paul says in 1 Corinthians 10:23, "All things are lawful [that is, permissible], but not all things are beneficial or advantageous. All things are lawful, but not all things are constructive [to character] and edifying [to spiritual life]" (AMP).

You can do anything you want; you have free will. But not everything is good for you.

Using social media without boundaries can be absolutely devastating. Devastating. You've probably already heard this. Maybe from your parents or your teachers or a coach. But it is so important that it's worth it for me to reiterate, remind, and plead with you.

A study was done in 2023 by Vivek Murthy, the US Surgeon General (the member of the President's cabinet who oversees public health and is known as the "Nation's Doctor"). This study showed that higher levels of social media usage are linked to adverse effects including depression, anxiety, poor sleep, low self-esteem, poor body image, body dysmorphia, and eating disorders. Murthy pointed to social media as the driving force of the teenage mental health crisis. Depression, sadness, and hopelessness have skyrocketed over the past decade.

There are hundreds of studies that show the exact same thing: excessive social media usage is linked to increased mental health issues. It's quite clear. **Why are**

we running back to something that isn't good for us? Proverbs 26:11 says, "Like a dog that returns to its vomit, is a fool who repeats his folly" (ESV).

And listen, I am with you in this struggle. I can get caught up in scrolling and being on these platforms way more than is good for me. And guess what? **When I spend too much time on social media, I personally feel the effects.** I feel more anxious and insecure, I compare myself to others more, and I become less content with the things that I have and who God created me to be (remember our talk about coveting?). I also don't sleep very well since my mind has been overstimulated (especially if I do it right before bed).

I'm not saying to get rid of your phone—although that is an option, I guess. But there are practical things you *can* do:

- Monitor your social media usage.
- Set a timer on your phone that restricts time on social media apps.
- Disable notifications so you don't feel like you need to check your phone every time you get a like, a comment, or follow.
- Get an accountability partner.

- Don't get on social media before bed, and don't get on social media first thing in the morning.

There are a lot of practical steps. These are just a few that I personally do.

And if this isn't a problem for you and you already have boundaries in place, praise God! I'm so proud of you. And so is God! **Maybe you can become the leader in your friend group and encourage others to have a better balance with this. Maybe you are the one who "calls them higher."**

Even if you don't struggle with this or don't use social media, be on guard with other things in your life. **Even a good thing can slowly become a god-thing (lowercase g) in our lives.** Sit with that thought for a little while . . .

God doesn't want you to live a life riddled with anxiety, fear, depression, hopelessness, and mental health challenges. Social media isn't the only culprit causing these things, but it's a big one. God wants more for you. And so do I.

Notes

CONCLUSION

I pray that you've been encouraged, empowered, and even lovingly challenged through this short devotional. While this devotional is a short read, I highly encourage you to read and reread it once a month or once every other month until these biblical truths and verses are implanted in your heart and mind and you walk in the freedom and truth God designed for you.

Maybe all of this seems new and strange to you. Maybe you've never taken the first step of placing your trust in Christ. If you'd like to invite (or reinvite) God into your life as Lord and Savior, say this prayer from your heart:

"Lord Jesus, I confess my sins and ask for your forgiveness. Please come into my heart as my Lord and Savior. Take complete control of my life and help me to walk in Your footsteps daily by the power of the Holy Spirit. Thank you, Lord, for saving me and for answering my prayer. Amen."

If you prayed that prayer, please connect with me on social media and shoot me a message! Let me know how this devotional encouraged you and what impacted you the most. I'd love to hear from you.

And remember that saying this prayer and inviting God into your life is just the first step. Find Christian friends, get plugged into your church, and join a Bible study. Start spending fifteen or twenty minutes every morning in prayer and reading the Bible. Start listening to worship music more than you do secular music. God doesn't just want a small piece of you, He wants *all* of you. And as it says in Ephesians 3:20, He can do more than you ask, think, or imagine . . .

Garrett

Printed in Great Britain
by Amazon